Robin Gill held the Michael Ramsey Chair of Modern Theology in the University of Kent, Canterbury for 20 years. Since 2013, he has been Emeritus Professor of Applied Theology there. For 13 years, he was chair of the Archbishop of Canterbury's Medical Ethics Advisory Group. He is Honorary Provincial Canon of Canterbury Cathedral and Canon Theologian at Gibraltar Cathedral. He is editor of the journal *Theology* and the Cambridge University Press monograph series, *New Studies in Christian Ethics*. Previously, he held the William Leech Research Chair of Applied Theology at the University of Newcastle. He is the author or editor of some 40 books, including *Health Care and Christian Ethics* (Cambridge University Press, 2007). His most recent are *Theology in a Social Context: Sociological theology volume 1, Theology Shaped by Society: Sociological theology volume 2,* and *Society Shaped by Theology: Sociological theology volume 3* (Ashgate, 2012–13) and *A Textbook of Christian Ethics* (4th edn, T&T Clark, 2014).

Little Books of Guidance
Finding answers to life's big questions!

Also in the series:

WHY DOES GOD ALLOW SUFFERING?

A little book of guidance

ROBIN GILL

First published in Great Britain in 2015

Society for Promoting Christian Knowledge
36 Causton Street
London SW1P 4ST
www.spck.org.uk

British Library Cataloguing-in-Publication Data
A catalogue record for this book is available from the British Library

ISBN 978–0–281–07540–9
eBook ISBN 978–0–281–07541–6

Typeset by Graphicraft Limited, Hong Kong
First printed in Great Britain by Ashford Colour Press
Subsequently digitally printed in Great Britain

eBook by Graphicraft Limited, Hong Kong

Produced on paper from sustainable forests

Contents

1

The problem

This little book reflects on a sharp tension between belief in an all-loving God and our experience of suffering. For some people this tension is a major stumbling block for Christian faith. It was so for one of the greatest British scientists, Charles Darwin.

It is often thought that it was science, and particularly the discovery of evolution, that caused Darwin to become an agnostic.

For a while as a young man he had considered a career in the Church. He had dropped out of studying medicine at Edinburgh University, and his freethinking father had almost persuaded him that the life of a country parson would suit him best. But he was transformed by his extraordinary voyage on HMS *Beagle* and spent the rest of his life as a scientist living on independent means.

His wife and first cousin, Emma, and their children went regularly to their local church in the Kent village of Downe. Charles Darwin remained friendly with successive vicars of Downe but seldom went to services there – a scientist and father of evolutionary theory apparently could not also be a Christian believer.

It is, however, much more likely that it was personal tragedy that triggered Charles Darwin's agnosticism. Even before their marriage Emma was concerned about Charles' religious doubts and feared for his eternal salvation. In a letter to him she reminded him of the text where Jesus says:

> Abide in me, and I in you. As the branch cannot bear fruit of itself, except it abide in the vine; no more can ye, except ye abide in me.
>
> I am the vine, ye are the branches: He that abideth in me, and I in him, the same bringeth forth much fruit: for without me ye can do nothing.
>
> If a man abide not in me, he is cast forth as a branch, and is withered; and men gather them, and cast them into the fire, and they are burned.   (John 15.4–6 KJV)

When his father died in 1848 Charles was in agony. If this text were literally true then it would appear that his sceptical father was now suffering the eternal punishments of hell. He had a serious breakdown with violent vomiting and deep depression. Three years later his beloved eldest daughter, Annie, died aged just ten. Understandably he described this as a 'bitter and cruel' loss. His hesitant religious faith was now buried with his dead child.

Perhaps you have chosen to read this book because you have experienced some similar personal tragedy yourself. Or perhaps, like many of us, you have seen parents devastated by the loss of a child. I don't remotely harbour Emma's fears about eternal punishment in hell (a particular phobia of the Victorians), but I do know just how traumatic funerals of young people can be. Taking such funeral services is deeply disturbing. Again and again parents say 'I expected to go first', and 'Why does God allow this to happen?'

Giving easy answers to grieving parents is the last thing any experienced minister or priest should do. We can hold hands and grieve with the bereaved; we can be alongside them in their weeping; we can offer words and prayers of comfort – all of this, but not facile 'explanations'. There is surely a proper time for grief and perhaps even for anger at God.

Yet once grief has abated there is also a proper time for reflection, and that is what this book is about. It will try to resist easy 'explanations' defending God, as well as those summarily dismissing God. It will suggest instead that careful reflection can reduce the tension between belief in God and experiences of innocent suffering.

Pain and suffering

First, though, it is important to make some clarifications. Pain and suffering are clearly related but there is a crucial difference between them: pain often has a beneficial function; it is not obvious that suffering does.

Listening carefully to doctors who specialize in pain control I have learned that they are divided among themselves. Some specialists are convinced that they can control pain without rendering a patient comatose; others are not. Yet all might agree that modern medicine has made considerable advances in pain control.

They might also add that individual patients have different pain thresholds. Some patients complain bitterly about pain that others either seem not to feel or simply endure without complaining. So most people want to have a local anaesthetic before having a tooth filled but some of us would rather have a small amount of sharp pain than two hours of numb jaw – there is a subjective element to pain.

'One leg', as he was later dubbed, showed a level of pain endurance that makes most of us wince. Henry William Paget, later the First Marquess of Anglesey, fought at Waterloo alongside the Duke of Wellington. Towards the very end of this fierce and bloody battle, Paget and Wellington were mounted alongside each other when Paget's right knee was shattered by grapeshot. Legend has it that Paget exclaimed: 'By God, sir, I've lost my leg!' and Wellington, removing his telescope briefly, simply responded 'By God, sir, so you have!'

Whether or not this verbal exchange was quite so stoical, a first-hand account of Paget's subsequent leg amputation (without a modern anaesthetic) is extraordinary:

> He never moved or complained: no one even held his hand. He said once perfectly calmly that he thought the instrument was not very sharp. When it was over, his nerves did not appear the least shaken and the surgeons said his pulse was not altered . . . He had no fever and surgeons say nothing could be more favourable.

For all his courage, Paget must have experienced serious pain. After all, he instantly knew he had a serious injury that needed attention if he was to avoid gangrene.

Insistent pain can be a clear warning that action is needed. If – much less dramatically than Paget – I have a thorn in my foot, pain quickly reminds me that I need to pull that thorn out as soon as possible.

Pain tells small children and animals that if they get too close to fire they get hurt. Without pain they would lose limbs – a real problem for those living with leprosy, a disease that numbs outer limbs. Pain also reminded the soldiers fighting at Waterloo that large-scale warfare is best avoided – it would be another century before the devastations of such warfare were experienced in Europe.

Physical pain in this sense is functional and beneficial – not all physical pain, of course, especially if there is nothing we can do about it. But for things we can fix, pain is important and useful.

Self-inflicted suffering

Another issue to clarify is self-inflicted suffering. The Battle of Waterloo was self-inflicted. Human beings do not have to fight wars and for most of the time, at least in the modern world, we settle disputes without going to war. The devastating wars that scarred the twentieth century – in which so many millions were killed – were manifestly self-inflicted. Despite reading several lengthy books on the subject I am still puzzled about what exactly caused the First World War. With hindsight it really does seem that this was a pointless and self-inflicted tragedy on a massive scale.

But why did God not intervene and stop wars happening? It is sometimes claimed that God could prevent human beings from fighting wars and could intervene whenever they are tempted to do so. Yet if free will is an essential part of moral choice (as I believe it has to be), it would be strange for God to intervene whenever we are tempted to use it for evil rather than good.

Again, as individuals we are quite adept at inflicting suffering on ourselves through smoking, drinking too much alcohol, exercising too little or eating too much unhealthy food. We disagree about what foods are currently healthy and how many units of alcohol it is responsible to drink. Nevertheless many of us could live more healthily than we do and, if we did, we might live longer and suffer less.

I wrote 'many of us' rather than 'all of us' because there do seem to be some people who, as a result of their genes or upbringing (neither of which they can change), are more prone to alcoholism or obesity than others. Healthy living is probably not a level playing field.

Yet if blame is to be apportioned, many of us might start with ourselves. It seems more appropriate for many of us to blame ourselves and not others – let alone God – for suffering that results from our own behaviour.

This is not to claim that a person who is suffering as a result of an unhealthy lifestyle should be denied compassionate care and treatment – if that were the case, most of us would be denied it on one ground or another. On the contrary, all those in need should be offered compassionate care and treatment no matter what the source of their suffering.

My point is simply this: it is odd to blame God for self-inflicted suffering, especially if we have a free will to change our behaviour. It is we ourselves who are finally responsible for much of the suffering caused by wars and unhealthy living.

Innocent and unwarranted suffering

It was not wars or unhealthy living that most troubled Charles Darwin. It was finally the suffering and early death of his beloved daughter. His agony started with the death of his father but that in turn was fuelled by a particular and all-too-human reading of Scripture. While many of us now reject the way he understood the Bible, we cannot escape the daughter. If anything, the suffering and death of a child in Western society today may shock us even more profoundly than in past eras. In Victorian England families might even have expected to lose some of their children through disease at an early age; today in the West we do not.

If you turn to the Bible and look in the book of Psalms this difference becomes evident. The authors of the Psalms often agonize about human suffering and especially about why it is that sinful people prosper while the innocent fall victim to oppression and injustice. Yet it is typically the suffering of adults that the Psalms have in mind – living with high infant mortality rates they would have expected some children not to survive. In that sense their world is different from ours. What they have in common with us, though, is a sense that God is answerable for innocent or unwarranted suffering:

> Why, O LORD, do you stand far off?
>> Why do you hide yourself in times of trouble?
> In arrogance the wicked persecute the poor –
>> let them be caught in the schemes they have
>>> devised . . .
>
> Their mouths are filled with cursing and deceit
>> and oppression;
>> under their tongues are mischief and iniquity.
> They sit in ambush in the villages;
>> in hiding-places they murder the innocent.
>
> Their eyes stealthily watch for the helpless;
>> they lurk in secret like a lion in its covert;
> they lurk that they may seize the poor;
>> they seize the poor and drag them off in
>>> their net.
>
> They stoop, they crouch,
>> and the helpless fall by their might.
> They think in their heart, 'God has forgotten,
>> he has hidden his face, he will never see it.'
>> (Psalm 10.1–11)

The focus here is on the suffering of the poor and the oppressed, and the complaint is that God has neglected them and, by default, let the wicked triumph. Charles Darwin cared just as passionately. Despite being otherwise a cautious and logical scientist he was also a compassionate human being who cared deeply about his dying daughter. And it was her suffering and death that finally undermined his belief in God. Many people today will identify with that.

It is innocent and unwarranted suffering – especially of children and animals – that many people in the West today find especially disturbing. This form of suffering raises serious questions about the nature and even the existence of God.

Acts of God

The philosopher Voltaire pointed caustically to another layer of innocent and unwarranted suffering. He was shocked by religious responses to the massive earthquake and tsunami that devastated Lisbon in 1755. This 'act of God' – as it is called in insurance policies – occurred on All Saints' Day. Many of the residents were worshipping in churches that collapsed on top of them. Altogether more than a third of the population was killed either by the earthquake or by the tsunami that followed. People watched with horror as buildings collapsed on their families; then they ran towards the coast to escape, only to be drowned by the tsunami. In his satire *Candide* Voltaire bitterly caricatured the Church's response:

> After the earthquake, which had destroyed three-fourths of the city of Lisbon, the sages of that country could think of no means more effectual to preserve the kingdom from utter ruin than to entertain the people with a [Ceremony

of the Inquisition], it having been decided by the University of Coimbra, that the burning of a few people alive by slow fire, and with great ceremony, is an infallible preventive for earthquakes. In consequence thereof, they had seized on a Biscayner for marrying his godmother and on two Portuguese for taking out the bacon of a larger pullet they were eating; after dinner, they came and secured Doctor Pangloss and his pupil Candide, the one for speaking his mind, and the other for seeming to approve what he had said . . . Candide was flogged to some tune while the anthem was singing; the Biscayne and the two men who would not eat bacon were burnt; and Pangloss was hanged, which was a common custom at these ceremonies. The same day there was another earthquake, which made most dreadful havoc. Candide, amazed, terrified, confounded, astonished, all bloody and trembling head to foot, said to himself, 'If this is the best of all possible worlds, what are the others?'

That final question raises a very important point about innocent and unwarranted suffering. Chapter 3 will return to it.

The Boxing Day tsunami in 2004 reminded the world that – God-given – forces of nature can indeed be very 'bitter and cruel'. Even if we remove the self-inflicted barbarities of the Inquisition parodied by Voltaire, the devastating effects of massive earthquakes and tsunamis remain. Why does God allow them?

The problem stated

The problem of unwarranted suffering – as I shall call it from this point on – can be stated quite simply:

If God is all-knowing, all-loving and all-powerful, why does God allow unwarranted suffering?

- If God is all-knowing then God should have been able to foresee the unwarranted suffering of humans and other sentient animals that would result from the creation of the universe.
- If God is all-loving then God would not wish humans or other sentient animals to have such suffering.
- If God is all-powerful then God would have been able to prevent such suffering when creating the universe.

So since unwarranted suffering obviously exists, then either God is not all-knowing, all-loving or all-powerful, or God does not actually exist.

2

Questionable explanations

There are several obvious ways of trying to resolve the problem of unwarranted suffering: we can deny one or other attributes ascribed to God; we can deny that only God created the universe; we can deny the existence of unwarranted suffering or the existence of God – or we can deny that the problem is quite as logical as it seems. In what follows I am going to give a measure of support only for the last of these options.

Denying attributes ascribed to God

(Note that I reiterate in this section the three points from my statement of the problem at the close of the last chapter.)

All-knowing?

'If God is all-knowing then God should have been able to foresee the unwarranted suffering of humans and other sentient animals that would result from the creation of the universe.'

Perhaps God is not really all-knowing. Psalm 10 suggests that the wicked at least have come to that conclusion: 'God has forgotten, he has hidden his face, he will never see it' (verse 11). And even the psalmist appears to be convinced that God needs to be reminded about how to behave appropriately.

There is a childish form of prayer that lists matters that people think God needs to be reminded about. They want to make sure God remembers those they love rather than bringing those they love into the presence of God, who already loves them.

A more persuasive objection is that God could not know something that is in principle unknowable – for example, something that is by its nature purely random. When builders mix sand and cement they will know the right proportions for a particular job. But they will have no idea where in the mixture any particular grain of sand will end up – it could go anywhere in it or even drop out altogether. Its path is random and depends on too many factors to be knowable.

So perhaps the unwarranted suffering of humans and other sentient animals was simply unknowable – even to an all-knowing God when creating the universe. Or perhaps an all-knowing God could have known but just happens to be fallible.

Perhaps. Yet this is not very persuasive – least of all the idea of a fallible God. The gods of the ancient Greeks were indeed fallible and are now usually regarded as just farcical.

All-loving?

'If God is all-loving then God would not wish humans or other sentient animals to have such suffering.'

Perhaps God is not all-loving. Psalm 10 suggests that God hides and stands off when faced with wicked people. That does not fit well with an all-loving God. Other parts of the Bible appear to present God as angry, vengeful and even spiteful. When as a young teenager I read through the entire Bible for the first time, I was particularly shocked by this story about the prophet Elisha:

He went up . . . to Bethel; and while he was going up on the way, some small boys came out of the city and jeered at him, saying, 'Go away, baldhead! Go away, baldhead!' When he turned round and saw them, he cursed them in the name of the LORD. Then two she-bears came out of the woods and mauled forty-two of the boys.   (2 Kings 2.23–24)

Even at that age I could see that a fundamentalist reading of Scripture was not for me. This savage punishment of the small boys, in the name of the Lord, seemed to be grossly disproportionate. If God really was thought to be behind the punishment then this was not the God I believed in. A spiteful God might indeed deliberately create a world of unwarranted suffering, but not my God.

Again there is a better way of understanding 'all-loving'. Parents will know that love sometimes needs to be tough love. Giving our children everything they want soon spoils them – sometimes we need to say 'no'. Sometimes we even need to let our children suffer in order for them to learn for themselves that excess can lead to suffering. We also need to punish them when they hurt other people.

Yet having conceded all that, the unwarranted suffering of small children and animals still seems deeply questionable. It looks all too like the mauling inflicted by those fearsome she-bears (I have seen one snarling at me in the Canadian Rockies – fortunately when I was in a car).

All-powerful?

> 'If God is all-powerful then God would have been able to prevent such suffering when creating the universe.'

Perhaps God is not all-powerful. This might be because there is another equal but evil power; or it might simply be because God's own power is finite. As a result God might not have been able to prevent unwarranted suffering when creating the universe.

Taking the second of these two options, would a finite God really be God? And would such a God be able to create the universe? Most Christians, Jews and Muslims have concluded otherwise. For them God is all-powerful or, better, almighty.

Here too there is an important point to make. To say that God is almighty is not to say God can make impossible things possible – for example, make two-plus-two add up to five. If something is in principle impossible then a divine fiat cannot make it possible.

But is the prevention of unwarranted suffering really impossible? At first sight it does not seem so. That is the force of Candide's outcry: 'If this is the best of all possible worlds, what are the others?' It doesn't seem that difficult to think that unwarranted suffering could have been eliminated – or at least reduced – in the world had the universe been created differently. The next chapter will take a second look at this point.

Denying only God created the universe

Perhaps instead God's power is limited by another equal but evil power. In Judaeo-Christian mythology the obvious candidate here is Satan or the devil. An evil power struggles with an all-loving God, so whereas God intends only whatever is loving and good, the evil power intends and effects the opposite, and it is not God who inflicts unwarranted suffering in the world but Satan. God and Satan, on this understanding, can be seen as co-creators of the universe.

Something like this seems to be suggested in a first reading of the opening chapter of the book of Job in the Old Testament. At the outset of this story – or better, parable – Job is depicted as 'blameless and upright' and prosperous. But then:

> One day the heavenly beings came to present themselves before the LORD, and Satan also came among them. The LORD said to Satan, 'Where have you come from?' Satan answered the LORD, 'From going to and fro on the earth, and from walking up and down on it.' The LORD said to Satan, 'Have you considered my servant Job? There is no one like him on the earth, a blameless and upright man who fears God and turns away from evil.' Then Satan answered the LORD, 'Does Job fear God for nothing? Have you not put a fence around him and his house and all that he has, on every side? You have blessed the work of his hands, and

his possessions have increased in the land. But stretch out your hand now, and touch all that he has, and he will curse you to your face.' The LORD said to Satan, 'Very well, all that he has is in your power; only do not stretch out your hand against him!' So Satan went out from the presence of the LORD.   (Job 1.6–12)

As a result Job loses all of his children, his property and even his health. So apparently it was Satan who was to blame for this unwarranted suffering, not God. God created the good in the universe but Satan created the evil.

On a second reading this is not so clear. In the parable Satan is given permission by the Lord to do these things. And once his suffering begins, Job's stoical response is to fall down and worship, saying: 'Naked I came from my mother's womb, and naked shall I return there; the LORD gave, and the LORD has taken away; blessed be the name of the LORD' (Job 1.21).

In other words he recognized that power ultimately still resides with God, not with Satan. In Judaeo-Christian mythology Satan has been considered a part of God's creation and not some independent power. As a result the notion of Satan or the devil does nothing to resolve the problem of unwarranted suffering.

Interestingly Job ignores Satan altogether in response to his own suffering. In the initial two chapters of the book, Job stoically defends God against criticisms from his wife: 'Shall we receive the good at the hand of God, and not receive the bad?' (2.10). So in the final resort it is apparently God who inflicts evil and unwarranted suffering on living creatures.

Denying the existence of unwarranted suffering – or of God

There is one way of reversing this conclusion – by claiming that evil and unwarranted suffering are an absence of good, not 'things' in themselves. God created every 'thing' and everything that God created is good. So what is not good is not part of creation but an absence within creation. On this understanding both evil and unwarranted suffering are illusions. Alternatively it is God who is the illusion.

We might wish to take a further step and distinguish between evil and unwarranted suffering, and claim that suffering – properly understood – is always warranted. Warranted suffering is no illusion. It is necessary either for our protection – as already seen with pain – or to develop our characters and prepare us for heaven.

Here again there are serious problems. For many today these medieval 'solutions' will be unacceptable. Faced with the indescribably shocking acts, say, of Fred and Rosemary West (including the torture and murder of their daughter for their own sadistic gratification), it feels both inadequate and insensitive to describe such evil as an 'illusion'. And not many of us today will be persuaded that the suffering of small children and animals is justifiable as a means of preparing them for eternal life.

So we might be tempted simply to dispense with God altogether.

Denying that the problem is quite as logical as it seems

This, in full, is how the problem of unwarranted suffering was stated at the end of Chapter 1:

> If God is all-knowing, all-loving and all-powerful, why does God allow unwarranted suffering?
>
> - If God is all-knowing then God should have been able to foresee the unwarranted suffering of humans and other sentient animals that would result from the creation of the universe.
> - If God is all-loving then God would not wish humans or other sentient animals to have such suffering.
> - If God is all-powerful then God would have been able to prevent such suffering when creating the universe.
>
> So since unwarranted suffering obviously exists, then either God is not all-knowing, all-loving or all-powerful, or God does not actually exist.

It is the word 'all-' here that is especially confusing. It qualifies the words that follow it but does so in manner that makes them impossible to understand literally.

The problem of God-language was recognized by the great thirteenth-century theologian Thomas Aquinas. When talking about God we typically use human terms, but by doing so we stretch their meaning. So when depicting God as 'father' or 'king' we are using terms drawn from our human experience of fathers and kings and saying there are some aspects of God that have affinities with them. We do not mean literally that God is a human father or an earthly king; rather we are using the words as analogies or metaphors to depict God, who is always beyond our all-too-human words.

Similarly when depicting God as 'love' we use a term drawn from our human-to-human relationships. We are not saying that God loves us in the same way we love our children; rather we are claiming that God's love has some affinity with human love but is not to be reduced to it.

Using everyday analogies to depict levels of reality that are beyond literal description is also a feature of micro- and macro-science. At the micro level, electrons behave differently from anything in our everyday experience. As a result, scientists depicting them sometimes refer to them as particles and sometimes as waves – they are neither and both. Similarly at macro level, infinite space defies everyday spatial depictions. Theologians are not alone in using analogies rather than literal depictions.

To make matters even more confusing, the problem stated above depicts God as not just 'loving' but 'all-loving'. So a human term is first applied analogically to God and then given an indefinite qualifier as well. The analogy itself is stretched to a point where it exceeds anything else in our experience. God is depicted not just as loving, very loving or very, very loving, but as *all*-loving.

In addition the stated problem does exactly the same to two other analogies applied to God. So it now depicts God as *all-knowing*, *all-loving* and *all-powerful* – as if that combination were self-explanatory.

It does all of this and uses the word 'then' to proceed – as if everyone will understand exactly what these qualified, analogical terms mean and entail. But this literal process works only if we are talking about a human being in literal terms. Instead we are trying to talk about God in terms that are both analogical and indefinitely qualified.

At this point in the discussion we might simply shrug our shoulders and say: 'There is nothing more to be said. We can never know what these terms mean or entail. End of discussion.'

That would be premature. There are two important theological areas still to consider. The first is about creation and the second is about Jesus. Neither will produce a knock-down argument to 'explain away' unwarranted suffering – but they can deepen our reflection and might even help us understand God a little better. This will be the task of the next two chapters.

3

Creation

It is time to dig a bit deeper. This chapter returns, as promised, to the paragraph in the previous chapter that made the following point:

> 'But is the prevention of unwarranted suffering really impossible? At first sight it does not seem so. That is the force of Candide's outcry: 'If this is the best of all possible worlds, what are the others?' It doesn't seem that difficult to think that unwarranted suffering could have been eliminated – or at least reduced – in the world had the universe been created differently.'

This is a really crucial issue in the problem of unwarranted suffering. If it is true that God *could have acted otherwise* and created a universe with less – or even no – unwarranted suffering, why did God not do so? Those words in italics are crucial.

The point this chapter will make is that it is actually much more difficult to establish that an all-loving God could indeed have acted otherwise than many people realize. Or to respond to Candide: 'This may not be the only possible world, but it may be the only world possible that could allow for the emergence of life possessing rational and moral choice.'

The book of Job is again helpful at this point.

Job's friends

The long poetic section of Job, stretching from the third to the middle of the final chapter, has been seen by many commentators as the most profound meditation on suffering in the Bible – or indeed in any great work of ancient literature. It takes human suffering very seriously indeed and explores several of the arguments noted in the previous chapter. And in its concluding chapters it offers a new challenge about our understanding of creation – or rather our lack of it.

It begins with an awkward transition. Just four verses after refusing to follow his wife's advice to 'Curse God, and die' (2.9), Job 'cursed the day of his birth' (3.1). From this point onwards Job complains about God's actions again and again. His earlier stoical acceptance of both good and bad coming from God is quickly forgotten.

There is a fractious debate from now until the end of chapter 31 between Job and his three 'friends' Eliphaz, Bildad and Zophar. They repeatedly argue that Job's sufferings *are* warranted and are a direct result of his wickedness. Job, by contrast, maintains his innocence and repeatedly blames God for inflicting unwarranted suffering on him.

The friends get increasingly explicit about the nature of Job's 'wickedness'. Eliphaz, in particular, itemizes it in his third speech:

> Is not your wickedness great?
>   There is no end to your iniquities . . .
> You have given no water to the weary to drink,
>   and you have withheld bread from the hungry . . .
> You have sent widows away empty-handed,
>   and the arms of the orphans you have crushed.
>
>   (Job 22.5–9)

Job insists this is not so. Instead he uses another argument noted in the previous chapter, namely to qualify or even reject the idea that God is all-loving.

So in response to Bildad's first speech, Job recognizes that God 'is wise in heart, and mighty in strength' (9.4) but also that God 'multiplies my wounds without cause' (9.17). Or, to express this in terms of the problem of unwarranted suffering: God is all-knowing and all-powerful but not all-loving. This argument works, albeit at God's expense.

Just as the friends are increasingly frank about Job's 'wickedness', so Job in turn is increasingly frank about God's shortcomings. He complains that God 'has torn me in his wrath, and hated me; he has gnashed his teeth at me' and 'shows no mercy' (16.9, 13). He claims that 'there is no justice' (19.7), asks 'what profit do we get if we pray to him?' (21.15) and confesses 'I am terrified at his presence' (23.15). Finally he declares to God, 'You have turned cruel to me' (30.21) – not at all edifying but remarkably modern in tone. It is a wail of grief and anger sounding through the ages.

Elihu intervenes

At this point the young Elihu enters the parable. He is angry with the three older friends and also with Job. The friends are blamed 'because they had found no answer' (32.3) and Job is blamed because he had added 'rebellion to his sin' (34.37).

On first reading this seems unfair. The friends might have thought they *had* provided an answer, namely that Job's suffering was a direct result of his wickedness. They might also have noticed that Elihu was making the same claim.

Yet a deeper reading suggests two new points being made by Elihu. The first is directed at Job. God, Elihu insists, 'sees all their steps' (34.21) *and* is 'righteous and mighty' (34.17). Unlike Job, therefore, Elihu does believe in God's essential goodness. Or, again, to express this in modern terms: in addition to being all-knowing and all-powerful, God, despite appearances, is also all-loving.

There is an obvious tension here and Elihu's other new point is crucial. It is simply this: does Job – or even his three friends – really understand what is involved in creation?

> Do you know how God lays his command upon
>   them,
>   and causes the lightning of his cloud to shine?
> Do you know the balancings of the clouds,
>   the wondrous works of the one whose knowledge
>   is perfect,
> you whose garments are hot
>   when the earth is still because of the south wind?
> Can you, like him, spread out the skies,
>   unyielding as a cast mirror?   (Job 37.15–18)

Job admits the limits of his knowledge

The great denouement of the parable has been reached. The voice of God speaks to Job. And Job in turn is humbled:

> Then the LORD answered Job out of the whirlwind:
> 'Who is this that darkens counsel by words
>   without knowledge? . . .
> Where were you when I laid the foundation of
>   the earth?
>   Tell me, if you have understanding.
> Who determined its measurements – surely you
>   know!
>   Or who stretched the line upon it?
> On what were its bases sunk,
>   or who laid its cornerstone
> when the morning stars sang together
>   and all the heavenly beings shouted for joy?'
>   (Job 38.1–7)

For four lyrical chapters of this profound parable the voice of God challenges Job. Does he really understand just what is involved in the act of creating the universe? And if he does not, why is he challenging God?

Finally Job relents: 'I have uttered what I did not understand, things too wonderful for me, which I did not know' (Job 42.3).

Scientists who admit the limits of knowledge

In an age of science it is tempting to shrug our shoulders again – this time at Job's admission of ignorance. Surely physicists and scientific cosmologists can tell us not just when the Big Bang occurred but also why it occurred – *and* how it might have occurred differently. Surely we can now do better than Job.

There does seem to be a scientific consensus today, both that the universe started with a Big Bang and that this can be approximately dated. Only a generation ago some distinguished scientists championed a Steady State theory according to which there was no such beginning – and therefore, some claimed, no need for a creator God. Today, however, Big Bang is widely accepted instead.

Yet this consensus about Big Bang does not extend to why the universe occurred – this might not even be a scientific question – *or* to whether it might have occurred differently. But a positive answer to the latter is essential to the problem of unwarranted suffering.

So far in this book I have written without my usual habit of cluttering it with quotations from other academics. At this point, however, I do need to quote two physicists with much more scientific credibility than I could ever muster.

John Polkinghorne's life has been divided into two remarkable careers. The first was as a scientist, culminating as Professor of Mathematical Physics at Cambridge University, and the second, starting in middle age, has been as an Anglican priest and author of many books on theology and science. He writes as follows:

> We all tend to think that had we been in charge of its creation, we would somehow have contrived it [the creation] better, retaining the good and eliminating the bad. The more we understand the delicate web of cosmic process, in all its

subtle interlocking character, the less likely it seems to me that that is in fact the case. The physical universe, with its physical evil, is not just the backdrop against which the human drama, with its moral evil, is being played out, so that the two can be disentangled. We are characters who have emerged from the scenery; its nature is the ground of the possibility of our nature. Perhaps only a world endowed with both its own spontaneity and its own reliability could have given rise to beings able to exercise choice.

(*The Faith of a Physicist*, pp. 84–5)

Clearly Polkinghorne has a theological axe to grind. Stephen Hawking does not but he too concluded, in *A Brief History of Time*, that given its complexity in developing life, this might well be the only universe possible. I cannot begin to evaluate their claims, yet it does seem odd that so many people, without being physicists themselves, apparently find it so easy to imagine that an alternative, free-from-suffering universe is possible.

Again John Polkinghorne concludes:

The fact is that our actual knowledge of the causal structure of the physical world is still patchy and incomplete . . . What the lengthy discussions [between scientists and theologians] in the 1990s on divine action did achieve was the important gain of making it clear that science had not established the causal closure of the world, as if what happens could be fully understood simply in physicalist terms.

(*Science and Providence*, p. xii)

Another scientist who makes important points in this area is Tom McLeish. He is Professor of Physics at Durham with particular research specialization in molecular theory of complex fluid flow – again well beyond my competence!

He writes about all sorts of areas in science, from astrophysics through climate science to quantum physics, where increasingly it is recognized that randomness or chaos is present alongside or within natural order. He relates this combination of chaos and order to attitudes to the natural world that are to be found in many parts of the Bible. At some points God is depicted as creating order from chaos but at others as being directly responsible for major acts of chaos – causing floods, earthquakes and so forth. MacLeish too looks to the closing chapters of Job to resolve this dilemma and to produce a theological understanding of chaos – as an opportunity for change – that can mesh with order and then relate strongly to scientific understandings of chaos and order:

> The message of Job is that chaos is part of the fruitfulness of creation; we cannot hope to control it any more than we can bridle Leviathan, but by understanding we might channel it. Indeed new structures can arise when we do – the 'beginning of wisdom' is not to double-lock the casket of our ignorance, but to 'seek the fear of the Lord', where this is understood to be a participation in a creator's deep insight into the structure of what he has made . . . situating our science and technology within a story of participative healing. (*Faith and Wisdom in Science*, p. 256)

A blunt conclusion

There are at least three different conclusions we might reach at this stage in the discussion. The first is rather vague, the other two are rather blunt.

The vague conclusion is that we may never be able to tell whether or not this is the only world possible that could allow for the emergence of life possessing rational and moral choice. We must remain agnostic on this issue: there might be an all-knowing, all-powerful and all-loving creator God but there might not – we will never know one way or another so further thought is pointless.

This is a position that quite a number – but still not a majority – of people have taken over the last 300 years. It is also a position many of us will understand: doubt cautions against fanaticism and is an important part of the modern mind.

Yet in the context of the problem of unwarranted suffering, this agnosticism is hardly relevant. The problem is driven by a conviction that the world as we know it – which includes suffering – *really could have been otherwise*. Once that conviction is weakened, the wind is taken out of the problem of unwarranted suffering.

The second conclusion is blunter. It states that if it is the case that the universe could not have been otherwise then an all-loving God should never have created it in the first place. Better to have no universe at all than one that contains earthquakes, tsunamis, floods, diseases and gross malformations. The world as we know it is an awful place; God – if there is a God – should never have allowed it to happen.

Some people reach that conclusion when they or someone they love are deeply depressed or terminally ill. They then might be tempted to commit suicide or seek assisted dying. Some parents with desperately ill or disabled children long for their death. But most do not, and many conclude that even a short life is to be treasured. And overwhelmingly most of us, even those with serious disabilities, conclude that this world is not such an awful place. Most of us value our existence and want to live tolerable lives as long as possible.

The third conclusion is almost as blunt. It states that this is indeed the only world possible that could allow for the emergence of life possessing rational and moral choice. So we simply have to put up with it. It can be tough in this world but there is, and never was, an alternative. Our response to those who are suffering is simply, 'Sorry, but that is the way things had to be.'

However, that isn't the approach Jesus took. The next chapter will look to him for a more compassionate approach to suffering.

4

Jesus and suffering

The New Testament does not offer an 'explanation' of unwarranted suffering. Instead it sets out to show that Jesus Christ, the Son of God, suffered as a man in the same way as ourselves even though he was without sin. More than that, Jesus lived for others to the point of suffering and dying for them. God, so Christians believe, really does care for us – so much so that God's Son suffered and died for us.

In some of the apocryphal gospels that were excluded from the New Testament canon, Jesus, as the Son of God, did not really suffer or die. In the belief that God could not suffer, they claimed that Jesus Christ only *appeared* to suffer and die on the cross. By contrast, the Gospels of Matthew, Mark, Luke and John insist that Jesus did both suffer and die, just as other human beings suffer and die.

In the New Testament Gospels, Jesus' life was focused on human suffering. He personified compassionate care towards those who suffer in two distinct ways: through his healing ministry and teaching; through his own suffering and death on the cross on our behalf.

The implication of this specifically Christian claim for the problem of unwarranted suffering is important. It maintains that even though this may be the only possible universe in which rational, free life could have emerged, God does care deeply about the suffering that has resulted. More than that: in and through Jesus, God has shared our suffering.

Jesus' ministry to those who suffer

As they were leaving Jericho, a large crowd followed him. There were two blind men sitting by the roadside. When they heard that Jesus was passing by, they shouted, 'Lord, have mercy on us, Son of David!' The crowd sternly ordered them to be quiet; but they shouted even more loudly, 'Have mercy on us, Lord, Son of David!' Jesus stood still and called them, saying, 'What do you want me to do for you?' They said to him, 'Lord, let our eyes be opened.' Moved with compassion, Jesus touched their eyes. Immediately they regained their sight and followed him.   (Matthew 20.29–34)

Many of the healing stories in Matthew, Mark and Luke begin as this story does. A vulnerable person – here two people – sees Jesus nearby and calls out for 'mercy' or 'pity' and Jesus responds. In this particular story from Matthew the two blind men are highly persistent, so much so that the crowd becomes angry. The men in turn shout again, emphasizing their plea for 'mercy' even more forcefully.

Neither the word 'mercy' nor 'pity' quite capture the sense of the Greek word used here. 'Mercy' in English usually carries ideas of judgment and justice as it does sometimes in Greek. The prisoner, once found guilty, pleads for 'mercy' from the judge before sentence is pronounced. Guilt has already been established so a plea for mercy is a plea for lenient punishment. This is seldom appropriate for healing stories in the Gospels. Guilt and sin are seldom mentioned in these stories.

'Pity' also presents problems in English. It can seem rather patronizing. When we pity someone we typically do so from a position of privilege. We pity the poor or people with serious disabilities because we, thankfully, are not poor or have no such disabilities. Those who are poor or disabled, on the other hand, may not be quite so grateful for our pity. They might well prefer our respect.

For these reasons some biblical scholars argue that it is more appropriate to use the English word 'compassion' to translate the Greek word used by the blind men in Matthew's story. So their plea to Jesus becomes instead: 'Have compassion for us, Lord, Son of David!'

That does fit Jesus' response in this story – he was 'moved with compassion'. This time the more usual Greek verb for 'compassion' is used. In Greek it has a highly visceral meaning, referring to the guts or entrails – something rather stronger than 'gut feeling', more like 'his guts or entrails heaved'. In the ancient world the guts were often thought to be the location of our deepest emotions.

The Latin from which the word 'compassion' itself is derived captures some of this meaning. It can be translated as 'suffering alongside' someone or even feeling 'with passion'. This is not just empathy, trying to put yourself into someone else's shoes; it involves action as well as feeling. If I claim to be compassionate about those in need but do nothing for them, others are likely to consider me not really compassionate at all.

Compassion properly understood involves three inter-linked responses: identifying someone as being in real need; feeling strongly for that person; then being determined to help that person in any way possible.

Understood in this way, compassion and justice are two sides of the same coin. If compassion tends to focus on needy people nearby, justice has a wider concern for the needy across the world.

A visit

Many years ago I visited an elderly couple in the rural parish where I was a new minister. They said they were pleased to see me and that it was a long time since they had had a visit from a vicar. They wished me well but explained why they could not come to church: 30 years earlier they had lost their only son when he was just 18. He was a strong swimmer and, as young people do, had attempted to swim in the local river when it was in full flood. Tragically, he drowned. The couple were still bitter about this and just could not see 'why this had to be'. As for Darwin, so for them this dreadful death simply did not make any sense; nor did it square up with any belief in a loving God.

I have no idea whether I helped them or not. Not remotely do I believe that this tragedy 'had to be', nor that God micromanages the world in this way. God, so I believe, gives us freedom even to do foolish things like swimming in a river in full flood. I wanted to help them move on, and treasure and give thanks for a life they loved so dearly – perhaps even to pray. But I feared they were stuck with Job's blunt complaint: 'what profit do we get if we pray to him?'

Yet since that visit I have met other couples whose faith has given them strength in their deep loss. For them, discarding God makes suffering even more pointless. It achieves little beyond making their lives even emptier and more meaningless. By contrast, their faith in God who shares their suffering gives them strength now and also a hope of future life beyond death.

For them this is not some false comfort or wishful thinking – as so many sceptics suppose – but faithful living in the presence of God. Such faithful living does not answer all of their doubts. But the same is true of doubts within a long, faithful marriage. Faithful living is about trusting the other despite doubts, for better and for worse. And it is about trusting God for better and for worse, in good times as well as bad.

Some people see suffering as a test of our faith by God. As we have seen, that is how the book of Job starts. Frankly I don't share that position. I see it the other way around: a mature faith in God sees beyond suffering, just as Gordon Wilson's did.

Gordon Wilson

After all the pointless suffering during the quarter century of troubles in Northern Ireland, the extraordinary faith of Gordon Wilson (1927–95) is still remembered. He was a lifelong Methodist and made his living as a draper at Enniskillen in Northern Ireland. One day in 1987 he and his daughter Marie, a nurse, took part in a Remembrance Day service around the local war memorial. Unbeknown, of course, to them, the IRA had planted a massive bomb there. When it was detonated Gordon and Marie were buried in the rubble; both were pulled from it but Marie died soon afterwards.

People around the world were deeply shocked by this act of terror targeting innocent people taking part in a religious ceremony. But Enniskillen is now better remembered for the truly remarkable words Gordon Wilson spoke at the time in an interview with the BBC. This is what he said about his lovely daughter as they lay buried in the rubble:

> She held my hand tightly, and gripped me as hard as she could. She said, 'Daddy, I love you very much.' Those were her exact words to me, and those were the last words I ever heard her say . . . But I bear no ill will. I bear no grudge. Dirty sort of talk is not going to bring her back to life. She was a great wee lassie. She loved her profession. She was a pet. She's dead. She's in heaven and we shall meet again. I will pray for these men tonight and every night.

This is truly remarkable faithful living in the presence of God despite immense personal suffering, a person of deep and mature religious faith seeing beyond unwarranted suffering.

Jesus on the cross

In his depiction of the final moments of Jesus on the cross (that barbaric weapon of torture the Romans used to punish and kill dissidents and criminals), Mark – and Matthew similarly – focuses on the words of apparent dereliction from the opening of Psalm 22:

> When it was noon, darkness came over the whole land until three in the afternoon. A three o'clock Jesus cried out with a loud voice, 'Eloi, Eloi, lema sabachthani?' which means, 'My God, my God, why have you forsaken me?'
>
> (Mark 15.33–34).

Luke is just as dramatic but his focus (in some ancient sources) is on words of trust and self-committal to God from Psalm 31: 'It was now about noon, and darkness came over the whole land until three in the afternoon . . . Then Jesus, crying with a loud voice, said, "Father, into your hands I commend my spirit"' (Luke 23.44–46).

John's Gospel is quite different. Here Jesus uniquely shows concern about his mother and the disciple he loved, and then:

> After this, when Jesus knew that all was now finished, he said (in order to fulfil the scripture), 'I am thirsty.' A jar full of sour wine was standing there. So they put a sponge full

of the wine on a branch of hyssop and held it to his mouth.
When Jesus had received the wine, he said, 'It is finished.'
Then he bowed his head and gave up his spirit.

(John 19.28–30)

In the original Greek 'It is finished' is represented by a
single word. The New English Bible translates it as 'It is
accomplished'; it could have been translated 'It is com-
pleted' or even 'It is fulfilled.' There is a sense of purpose
and direction in the Greek word that is missing from
'It is finished.'

This work of faithful living through suffering is now
complete. Jesus had lived for others to the point of suffering and dying for them.

In a troubled world of religiously inspired violence,
Jesus' dying on the cross needs careful treatment. Too
often in Christian history the idea of 'laying down one's
life for one's friends' has been used to depict warriors
risking their lives in battle. It is not too difficult to see
how it might also be used to depict suicide bombers,
especially those driven by religious conviction.

But the cross is emphatically not about Jesus taking
the lives of others. It is about Jesus giving his own life
for others without taking life at all. In this final act of
faithful living, Jesus fulfils the commandment to love
others: 'And this is eternal life, that they may know you,
the only true God, and Jesus Christ whom you have sent.
I glorified you on earth by finishing the work that you
gave me to do' (John 17.3–4).

Jesus identifies with those who experience unwarranted
suffering and takes that suffering to himself. Expressing

this from a God-centred perspective, John's Gospel captures it in a single verse – a verse that has brought strength
and support to many like Gordon Wilson who have
experienced or witnessed horrendous and unwarranted
suffering: 'God so loved the world that he gave his only
Son, so that everyone who believes in him may not perish
but may have eternal life' (John 3.16).

Further reading

1 The problem

The account of Darwin's source of agnosticism can be found in James Moore, *The Darwin Legend: Are reports of his deathbed conversion true?* (London: Hodder & Stoughton, 1995).

The account of Paget's amputation can be found in the Seventh Marquess of Anglesey's *One Leg: The life and letters of Henry William Paget, First Marquess of Anglesey, KG, 1768–1854* (London: Leo Cooper, 1996).

The quotation from Voltaire comes from the beginning of chapter 6 of his *Candide* and can be found at <www.bartleby.com/194/6.html> (accessed 2 May 2015).

2 Questionable explanations

There are many books on the problem of unwarranted or innocent suffering. C. S. Lewis's *The Problem of Pain* was first published in 1940 and is still in print with HarperCollins. Its language is accessible but now antique and its 'solutions' will not please all, yet it is still good on 'pain'. More sophisticated is John Hick's classic work *Evil and the God of Love* (London: Macmillan, 1966). A well-regarded anthology is Marilyn McCord Adams and Robert M. Adams (eds), *The Problem of Evil* (Oxford and New York: Oxford University Press, 1990).

On religious language there are also many books. However, I. T. Ramsey's *Religious Language* (London: SCM Press, 1957) is still instructive.

3 Creation

John Polkinghorne's *The Faith of a Physicist: Reflections of a bottom-up thinker* (Princeton, NJ: Princeton University Press, 1994) was first given as the Gifford Lectures for 1993–4. His *Science and Providence: God's interaction with the world* (London: SPCK) was first published in 1989 but the quotation here comes from the new Preface to the 2005 reprint.

Tom McLeish's *Faith and Wisdom in Science* (Oxford: Oxford University Press, 2014) I recommend very highly.

A lively and up-to-date defence of free will is given in Alfred R. Mele's *Free: Why science hasn't disproved free will* (Oxford: Oxford University Press, 2014).

4 Jesus and suffering

I explore Jesus' approach to healing further in my book *Health Care and Christian Ethics* (Cambridge: Cambridge University Press, 2006).